GYPSIES

Thomas Acton

Silver Burdett Company

Editor Diana Railton
Design Roland Blunk MSIA
Picture Research Caroline Mitchell
Production Rosemary Bishop

First published in 1981 by
Macdonald Phoebus Ltd
Holywell House
Worship Street
London EC2A 2EN

Adapted and published in the United States
by Silver Burdett Company, Morristown, N.J.
1982 Printing

ISBN 0-382-06645-6

Library of Congress Catalog No. 82-80194

Contents

The first Gypsies

'They scarcely ever stop in one place more than thirty days . . . they move from field to field with their oblong tents, black and low, like the Arabs', and from cave to cave.'
Simeon Simeonis, a monk visiting Crete in 1322

Right: These Gypsies have pitched their tents beneath the walls of a town in the Middle East. The tent they are using is designed to keep out the heat of the sun. To the left of the picture one woman is milking a goat, while another is rolling out dough for a kind of bread or savoury cake similar to Indian chapatis, and called *marikli*. The men are playing Three Stones, a game still played by Gypsies today.

Some Gypsy groups, like the Banjara, the Zott and the Halebi, remain in Asia to this day.

The ancestors of the Gypsies lived in north-west India over 1,000 years ago. There each person was born into a 'caste' or fixed class of society. The members of each caste did the same sort of job. The four main castes were priests, gentry, merchants and peasants. Below the peasants were the outcastes like sweepers and blacksmiths. A man was not allowed to marry a woman from a higher caste.

Nomads

Some lower-caste groups found they could earn a better living by becoming 'nomads'. India then was a wealthy country and people in the villages could pay for better pots, pans, jewellery and entertainment than they could make for themselves. So metalsmiths, entertainers and travelling traders toured the country, staying and working in each village in turn, until they had done as much business as possible.

Migration

From the fifth century onwards, Indian musicians travelled to Persia. Between AD 800 and 1000, a great stretch of land from northern India to southern Europe was conquered by a new religion, Islam, and governed as one country. Nomads from India plied their various trades all over this area. They lived mainly in tents. Their metalwork was stronger than that produced by the local people, and their music was attractive and different. Soldiers and even lords who had lost their land sometimes joined the nomads.

Outside India people from different castes had to band together more. These groups, who called themselves names like Rom or Zott, became the people whom we call Gypsies.

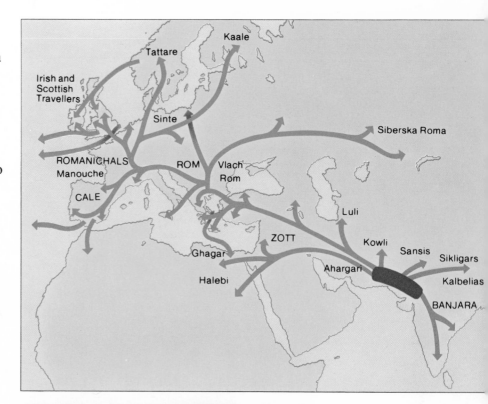

Above: This map shows the main routes of the Gypsies out of India up to about 1700. In Europe the greatest numbers stayed in East Europe (then ruled by Turkey) and were called 'Rom' which means 'men' in Romanes, the Gypsy language. Among those who went to North and West Europe, many called themselves 'Romanichals' which means 'Romani fellows'. In Spain and southern France they called themselves 'Calé', which means 'Blacks'. These names included hundreds of smaller groups. Non-Gypsies called them different names in each country, for example 'Gypsies' in England, 'Gitanos' in Spain.

Left: There are still many nomads in India today. Like the girl on the cover of this book, the man on the left is a modern Kalbelia nomad from Rajasthan in India. He is making a puppet to entertain people in the villages they pass through. The Kalbelias also entertain with snake-charming and music, and sell herbal medicines. Notice that the man is wearing earrings. Some Gypsies believe that wearing gold or silver earrings helps the eyesight. The Kalbelias make a lot of jewellery.

Entry into Europe

The Gypsies reached eastern Europe at a time when there were frequent wars between Christians and Muslims. Often Gypsy craftsmen were captured and enslaved, and forced to manufacture horseshoes, weapons and other goods for their new masters.

A Gypsy Duke or leader

Some Gypsies avoided slavery. In 1417 a group of about 200, led by a man called Andrew, reached the Emperor of Germany. They told him they had come from the Middle East (which the Germans then called 'Little Egypt'), and had escaped from the Muslims, who had made them give up Christianity. Now they wanted to become Christians again, and go on a pilgrimage around Europe. The Emperor gave Andrew a letter recognizing him as their 'Duke', and asking everybody to help them. Since the letter said they came from 'Little Egypt', people began calling them 'Egyptians' (even when they did tell some people they were Indians). The name stuck, and was shortened in English to 'Gypsy'.

Local reactions

At first most people were sympathetic to the refugees. Leaders like Duke Andrew dealt with local rulers as equals. They dressed in rich robes and looked just like other nobles. Some of their followers, however, looked very poor, and were dressed in blankets tied up with string. Older women told people's fortunes, and were accused of witchcraft and theft. Prejudice against Gypsies developed.

In Scotland Gypsies were welcomed until 1541, when King James V quarrelled with John Faw, 'Earl of Little Egypt', and ordered him out of the country.

Some travelling Gypsies catch up with others who are preparing a feast. The date is about AD 1600. The food is being carefully prepared to keep it clean. The feathers from the goose will be used to stuff a quilt. The tents beneath the tree are smaller and sturdier than those on page 5. This design, called the 'bender tent' by English Gypsies, is still sometimes used today. It is good for keeping out wind and rain. (See page 44 for details of how to make one.)

The great persecutions

'Their ears be nailed to a tree, and cutted off, and them banished the country; and if thereafter they be found again, that they be hanged . . . the idle people calling themselves Egyptians.'
Scottish law against vagrants, 1579

Life became hard for Gypsies in sixteenth-century Europe. Even before 1500, laws were passed to expel Gypsies from Spain and Switzerland. By 1650, most Gypsies were slaves or hunted outlaws, or else beggars hiding the fact that they were Gypsies.

Scapegoats

Generally during this period the rich became richer and the poor poorer. Prices went up but wages did not keep pace. Peasants were thrown off the land they had tilled.

When people are out of work, they often look round for someone to blame. Strangers make good scapegoats. In England there were riots against foreigners, and Queen Elizabeth I expelled all the freed Black slaves, and strengthened laws expelling Gypsies. But Gypsies had nowhere to go. Then laws were passed in England and elsewhere, condemning all Gypsies to death, as Hitler was to do in our own century (see page 14).

Who are the true Gypsies?

The Gypsies who escaped slavery had to mix with local people to survive, and to use the local language and customs. Different Gypsy groups grew apart, each one thinking itself the best. So, when Gypsies were accused of witchcraft or stealing, it was easy for them to say: 'It's not us – it's those others in the next town who pretend to be Gypsies. True Gypsies wouldn't do such a thing.' This didn't always save them from the gallows, but it built up a myth of there being 'true' and 'not true' Gypsies.

Today people still say they are not against 'true Gypsies', only 'Tinkers', without really knowing what they are saying.

Below: This picture of Gypsies comes from a Swiss book published in 1552. The head of the family sits having a meal with his wife, while around them their grown-up daughters tell the fortunes of curious passers-by. People believed this was magic. In fact it was mostly commonsense. The Gypsies threw out hints about the work and love-life of their customers and watched how they reacted. Fortune-tellers would guess that people were going on a journey, or give advice to the unhappy. But the church considered it was magic, and punished them as witches.

Left: At first in western Europe Gypsies were treated with great respect. In the sixteenth century this Gypsy healed the King of Scotland after his doctors had given up hope. Notice the look of calm authority on her face which led heraldist Jacques Leboucq to draw her.

Right: From the seventeenth century towns used to post notices like the one in this picture, showing Gypsies being hanged, to warn them to stay away. In western Europe Gypsies were hanged or flogged, or sent as forced labour to America. In eastern Europe Gypsy slaves were also beaten or mutilated, and families split up.

These Gypsies are being attacked for coming to town despite the notice. The local people probably think they are lucky to get away with being flogged only, and not hanged. In England, at York in 1596, magistrates made children watch while their parents were executed just because they were Gypsies. As late as 1725, at Zaltbommel in the Netherlands, Gypsies were tortured to death, and their heads cut off and placed on spikes to warn other Gypsies away.

Straff Zigeuner
Junner u immind ein

9

A Gypsy hero

'There is scarcely a farmhouse in Galloway where stories of his kindness are not still related.' **Andrew McCormick, 1905**

To escape persecution some Gypsies fled to the hills where few people lived; others mixed with unemployed vagrants looking for work. Some became soldiers, or found protection as the servants of rich landowners. Then, as persecution died down, they started their nomadic life again, trading from village to village and selling their wares. One Scottish Gypsy, called Billy Marshall, supposedly born in 1673, did all of these things. He was forced to join the army, but ran away and became the leader of a gang of Gypsies and outlaws in Galloway. They earned a living by protecting peasants' cattle from other outlaws.

General of a rebel army

In 1724 Billy Marshall joined a revolt of peasants and craftsmen from the town of Kirkcudbright. They formed an army to fight the local gentry, who were stealing common land and interfering with their trade and religion, and asked Billy Marshall to lead it. The government considered that this was revolution, and they sent in soldiers to crush the revolt.

Horn cups and spoons

Afterwards, Billy Marshall and others who escaped were on the run for 20 years. But in 1745 they earned a pardon from the government for fighting against Jacobite rebels. Able once again to work, they began to make spoons and cups from the horns of the cattle they were protecting, and sold them round the villages. Billy Marshall presented two horn spoons and a cup at the christening of the son of the Earl of Selkirk, who gave him a pension, and protected him. He died in 1792.

In the 1720s Galloway's rebellious peasants went out at night and pulled down the fences which the landowners had put up to keep the peasants' cattle from the common land. The peasants were joined by craftsmen from Kirkcudbright. They elected a council, set up their own government, and made Billy Marshall the general of their army.

The government sent a regiment of dragoons (cavalrymen) to fight them, but the rebel army looked so strong that the dragoons decided not to risk a battle. Instead the landowners were sent in to negotiate. This scene shows them approaching the rebels under a white flag of truce. There was no battle on this day, but the landowners offered so many concessions that most of the rebels gave up, and Billy Marshall was eventually defeated.

Billy Marshall stands at the front. Behind him
some of the peasants carry pitchforks and
scythes for lack of better weapons. The
Marshall family remember 'Outlaw Billy' as a
great man. He fought oppression when he
could, fled when he could not, compromised
when he had to; above all, he survived.

On the move again

'No, we were not always slaves; see our brothers who live in the mountains. They know nothing of chains, neck irons, whippings and hunger and thirst . . . Let us go free!'
Matéo Maximoff, a Rom novelist, writing about the slave revolts of his ancestors in Romania

Right: All through Europe, independently of each other, different Gypsy caravan designs were developed. The most highly decorative were built in England, such as this Reading waggon, made in about 1919 by the firm of Dunton. The Dunton family, like most builders of caravans, were not Gypsies, but worked to instructions from Gypsy clients.

Below: The inside of a Reading waggon. Notice the stove on the left-hand side and the bed at the back, with a cupboard beneath it. Notice also the gleaming metalwork.

By 1750 most remaining European Gypsies lived quietly. In the West they were mainly traders; in the East they were usually musicians or slaves. But from about 1750 onwards, the Industrial Revolution changed all this. New methods of manufacturing often meant that the work of Gypsy craftsmen, slave or free, was no longer needed. Social reformers and missionaries protested about the conditions endured by Gypsies. The slaves in south-east Europe – half the world's Gypsies – began to rebel, and some fled north to Russia or west towards America.

The Gypsy caravan

During the Industrial Revolution better roads and ships were built. On the new, hard roads Gypsies could travel further and use bigger and stronger vehicles. In the early nineteenth century the horse-drawn Gypsy caravan made its first appearance. The design was adapted from other vehicles such as farm carts, stage-coaches and even railway carriages. These caravans are usually thought of as 'traditional', but in fact they show how flexibly Gypsies react to a new situation.

Motorization

Not all Gypsies lived in horse-drawn caravans. Tents were still used, and some Gypsies rented or bought houses. In the 1950s road traffic became faster, and it was harder to find places for horse-drawn caravans to stop. Most nomadic Gypsies began to use modern aluminium caravans towed by lorries. These are more comfortable and convenient than the old wooden waggons. Today only a few poorer Gypsies live in tents or horse-drawn caravans.

Left: This very simple type of caravan was used by Rom in south-eastern Europe, and taken west by them. It is little more than a bender tent put on top of a farm cart.

Below left: This is a more elaborate waggon, called a Bow Top waggon, and used in Ireland and England.

Below: This French caravan is more unusual. Gypsy caravans do not often have a door at the side, as that is generally where the main bed is. The caravan may be based on an old builders' or road menders' waggon.

The Nazi holocaust

'I saw a woman guard kill four Gypsy children for eating leftover food.'
Barbara Richter, Auschwitz Gypsy prisoner Z 1963

During the 1930s many people were unemployed. As before, when life was hard, people searched for scapegoats. In several countries dictators came to power, offering what seemed like easy solutions. The most dangerous of these was Adolf Hitler, leader of the Nazi party in Germany.

Concentration camps

To begin with the Nazis made lists of all Gypsies, and confiscated their money. Then, if a person had any Gypsy blood, even a Gypsy grandparent, he or she was taken from school or army, home or factory, roadside or wood, and forced into a concentration camp. Many of the prisoners in these camps died from being overworked, or because they were used in medical experiments. Even more were killed in gas chambers.

An English Gypsy, Fred Wood, was in the British armed forces which liberated one concentration camp from the Nazis. He said: 'We faced something terrible. Heaps of unburied bodies and unbearable stench. When I saw the surviving Romanies (Gypsies), with small children among them, I was shaken. Then I went over to the ovens (where the dead bodies were burnt) and found on one of the steel stretchers the half-charred body of a girl, and I understood in one awful minute what had been going on there.'

Death squads

During the Second World War, the Nazis also killed Gypsies in other countries. Special troops roamed through Poland and the Soviet Union looking for Gypsies and Jews. They even asked for lists of Gypsy names so that these could be rounded up if they conquered England.

Below: These Sinte Gypsy men were imprisoned in Buchenwald concentration camp in Germany in 1938. They had to wear striped prison uniforms and a number was tattooed on their wrists. Today a few survivors still have these numbers. They were not guilty of any crime; they were imprisoned just because they were Gypsies, and Hitler and the Nazi party felt that they threatened Germany's 'purity'. In the camps they were given little food and had to work very hard. Some were infected with deadly diseases just to see what would happen.

Below: On Good Friday 1980, Herr Romani Rose (in the white raincoat) leads German Sinte Gypsies to carry wreaths into the site of the old concentration camp at Dachau. They are commemorating all the Gypsies murdered by the Nazi party in the period when they ruled Germany between 1933 and 1945. Some of the Gypsies have put on the old striped uniforms that prisoners had to wear in the camps.

Bottom of page: A small boy puts a flower on a mass grave in a concentration camp.

After the war

Altogether, between 250,000 and 500,000 Gypsies were killed by the Nazis, along with nearly 6 million Jews. After the war the Jews established the state of Israel, and were given compensation by the West German government, but Gypsies received nothing. Governments and police continued to persecute them. This encouraged Gypsies from many countries to get together to form the World Romani Congress.

Never again

The World Romani Congress has erected memorials to the dead Gypsies at the sites of some of the concentration camps. An English Gypsy schoolgirl, Rosemary Penfold, wrote after visiting one in 1972:

'We all went, as Roms, to put a wreath at the foot of the graves. The camp was the most terrible place I myself have ever been inside. Inside one of the buildings there were pictures which showed Roms and Gaujos (non-Gypsies) who were going to be killed. Some had no clothes on. Some were put in piles, their dead bodies were thrown into cellars, and they were burnt in another building. There were gas cells and there was a place where ashes were kept. This camp was high on the hills and no-one could get out.

'In my heart I had a weak point. I just had to cry. It was as if lots of eyes were looking at me. When we went inside I could sort of hear the cry of all those 12,000 Roms who died (there). Just think of it, 12,000! The men who killed them could not have been men. I ask you, could you kill 12,000 people? No, of course not, because you would feel guilty. So we must not let this happen ever again, because it could happen to us'.

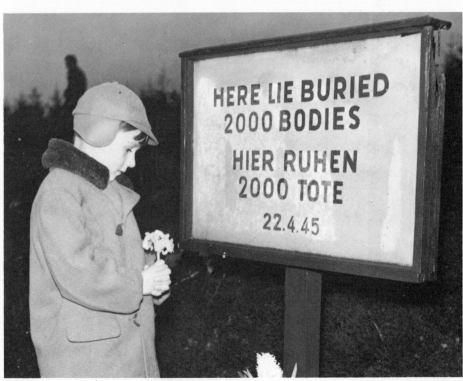

HERE LIE BURIED
2000 BODIES
HIER RUHEN
2000 TOTE
22.4.45

The survivors

'We are people of worth, not thieves or murderers. History has played with us, thrown us down and split us up. But we must seek our destiny . . . by coming together as one people.'
Jarko Jovanovic, at the World Romani Congress, 1978

Though most Gypsies today are settled in one place, some are still 'nomads'. The nomadic Gypsies usually travel only short distances inside a small area of one country; sometimes they have a house which they return to in winter. But others travel widely, sometimes even trading between the different continents.

Leadership

Each group of Gypsies is independent; there is no central Gypsy government. Within a group, every family makes its own decisions. In India the Banjara have 'naiks', headmen who judge disputes with the help of a small council of elders. Some Rom groups have a similar council, the *kris*, which is led by respected heads of family. When important decisions have to be made, or someone is accused of a crime, all members of the group are allowed their say. Offenders may be fined, or else treated as unclean by the rest of the group, who will refuse to speak to or eat with them. This affects some offenders so much that they become ill and die. Strong-minded Gypsies, however, can escape a quarrel by moving elsewhere to live as they please.

Gypsy kings and Gypsy councils

When Gypsies have to deal with non-Gypsy authorities such as governments, a special kind of representative is needed. It works best if this 'leader' knows both the Gypsy and the non-Gypsy world, like Duke Andrew for example (see page 6). Before 1939 some Gypsies even called themselves 'Kings'. They did not 'rule' the Gypsies, but tried to persuade governments to improve conditions for them. Nowadays this is done by organizations like the World Romani Congress.

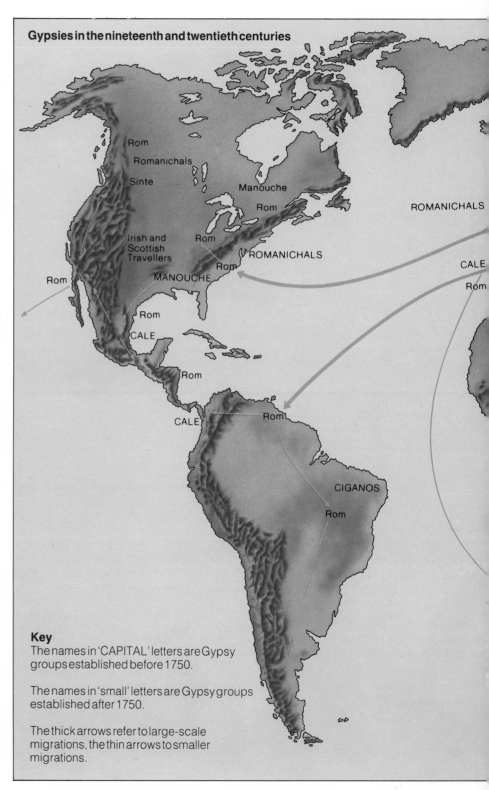

Gypsies in the nineteenth and twentieth centuries

Rom
Romanichals
Sinte
Manouche
Rom
ROMANICHALS
Irish and Scottish Travellers
Rom
MANOUCHE
Rom
Rom
Rom
CALE
Rom
CALE
Rom
CALE
Rom
CIGANOS
Rom
ROMANICHALS
CALE
Rom

Key

The names in 'CAPITAL' letters are Gypsy groups established before 1750.

The names in 'small' letters are Gypsy groups established after 1750.

The thick arrows refer to large-scale migrations, the thin arrows to smaller migrations.

Today there are estimated to be 10–12 million Gypsies outside India, and about 20 million nomads still in India. There are many groups, differing so much in language, customs and lifestyle that it is sometimes hard to recognize them as members of the same people.

Since the great migrations described on page 12, no country has just one group of Gypsies. Most Western countries have an 'old' group dating from about 1500, and a 'new' group dating from about 1850. Sometimes these groups despise each other, claiming to be the only 'true Gypsies'.

ATTARE
Rom
KAALE
Rom
Rom
Rom
ROM
ROM
Rom
SINTE
Rom
ANOUCHE
om
ROM
LULI
SINTE
Rom
om
ZOTT
KOWLI
Rom
HALEBI
SANSIS
ARHAGARI
KALBELIAS
BANJARA
Rom

Rom

Romanichals
Rom
Rom
Romanichals
Irish Travellers

Romanichals

17

Gypsy homes today

'Well, this policeman stopped my motor. He asked me where I lived. "First tree I come to I can climb, mate," I said.'
English Gypsy girl, 1972, *after being moved on*

Below: This Gypsy family have been pictured with their dogs by the back door of their house in one of the poorer suburbs of a French town. Thousands of Rom live on the outskirts of Paris in houses like this. The dogs have to stay outside in the backyard; letting them into the house itself would be considered unclean. Although the outside of Gypsy houses may look drab and ordinary, inside they are usually as richly decorated as the caravans of nomads, with glass cabinets full of gleaming crockery and colourful ornaments.

Almost all nomadic Gypsies now live in modern caravans pulled by lorries or vans. Their biggest problem is to find somewhere to park. Their old stopping places have gradually been built on or fenced off. In western Europe in the 1960s crisis point was reached: because Gypsies were always being driven on by police and officials, they had no time to earn a living.

Caravan sites

Some Gypsies began to fight back by sitting down in front of the bulldozers sent to tow away their caravans. An International Gypsy Committee was formed in Paris by Vanko Rouda and Vaida Voevod. Eventually governments began to provide official caravan sites; but there are not enough of them, few are attractive, and site regulations restrict the Gypsies' freedom. But they do at least provide security.

New houses and flats

The majority of the world's Gypsies do not and never did live in caravans. Instead they had a variety of other homes. Some Calé in Spain used to live in caves. Before 1945 the Boyash in Hungary lived in the forests, in holes dug under the roots of trees. After the war, however, the Hungarian government built new houses specially for them.

All over Europe, many Gypsies have always lived in houses. In the West they may not let their neighbours know they are Gypsies, for fear of prejudice. But in the old cities of eastern Europe there is often a recognized Gypsy 'quarter'. The biggest is the new town of Shuto Orisare, built after an earthquake at Skopje in Yugoslavia destroyed the old Gypsy quarter in 1963.

18

Below: English Gypsy caravans are still the most highly decorated in the world. This one has cut-glass windows, and streamlined chrome patterns on the walls. The Gypsies are using bottle-gas for cooking, but they still have a coal stove with a chimney. Water is kept in the churn by the door.

Bottom of page: The inside of a modern caravan belonging to a rich Gypsy family. It looks very similar to the old one shown on page 12. Not all Gypsies are as well-off as this.

Growing up Gypsy

'I was not able to go to school. So I said to myself "I will learn myself how to read proper." . . . Milestones, finger-posts (signposts) and most of all, the rubbish-dumps were my teacher.'
Johnny Connors, an Irish Traveller, 1972

Below: This Manouche Gypsy family are camping near the River Rhône in France. The girls have stopped washing the family's clothes for a minute to talk to the men who are eating a meal; perhaps they have walked away from the photographer! Their caravan, and the van used to pull it, are behind them. While they are still young, Gypsy boys and girls have to learn how to wash clothes and mind babies. Around half the Gypsy children in western Europe still do not go to school.

Like most people, Gypsies love children. When they are small, Gypsy children are allowed great freedom and are seldom smacked or beaten. But Gypsy parents do always teach their children to be clean, to respect their elders, and not to talk to strangers. Gypsies are not really considered grown-up until they have children of their own; they keep in close contact with their family and often work in partnership with them.

Learning Gypsy life

Life for Gypsies varies greatly according to the group they belong to, and the country they live in. In most Gypsy groups the jobs of men and women are different. In some groups the women go out to work, leaving the men behind; more often, it is the men who go out; and occasionally, especially with farm work, men and women work side by side.

Children learn by imitating their parents. They go out to work with them. They are taught how to cook and change nappies. Boys are generally given more freedom, and this can make girls envy them.

Learning to read and write

Until this century few people anywhere learned to read or write. When schooling was made compulsory, still very few Gypsy children went to school. Nomads did not stay long enough in one place; and some schools, out of prejudice, refused to accept Gypsy children. But in the past twenty years Gypsies and their supporters throughout Europe have struggled for the right to be educated. Special schools for Gypsy children have even been started. In eastern Europe almost all Gypsy children now go to school.

Below: This Rom Gypsy family in Turkey are travelling with two horse-drawn carts.

Bottom of page: This school in a caravan is on an official Gypsy caravan site in France. An English Gypsy, Julie Mitchell, wrote:
> 'My little brother goes to school
> and the boys do bully him
> and call him Gypsy Tramp
> and Thieves and he's only eight,
> and cries at the night.'

Some Gypsies, like Julie herself, love going to ordinary school; others need special help.

Marriage

'There is nothing of jumping over broomsticks or other tomfooleries that outsiders attribute to Gypsies. The ceremonial is the same as that of Rebekah and Isaac. Isaac brought Rebekah into his tent and she became his wife and he lived with her.'
Gypsy Rodney Smith, preacher, 1901

Marriage, the start of a new family, is very important to Gypsies. There are two main ways for Gypsies to get married. Most of the Rom and Asian groups have a 'bride-price' system; other groups marry by 'elopement'. Religious or civil ceremonies may be held instead of or as well as the Gypsy marriage. It is sometimes said that Gypsies will only marry other Gypsies. This is not true. Over the centuries all Gypsy groups have intermarried with non-Gypsies.

The bride-price system

Here it is the father's duty to find a suitable girl for his son to marry. Sometimes engagements are arranged for small children, but more often they wait until they are teenagers. A matchmaker may be called in to help, for a small fee. A few days before the wedding the boy's father pays the girl's father a 'bride-price' (ranging from perhaps £100 to £5000). Some of the money will be spent on the wedding party, and on bedding and crockery for the young couple.

The wedding party

The bride and groom are not supposed to see each other before their wedding day. On the day the groom comes with his family to collect the bride. Sometimes they pretend to have to capture her, and the bride has to look sad at leaving her family.

    The wedding is a great social occasion. Among the Arliski Rom, in Yugoslavia, feasting and dancing last for three days. Whole sheep are cut up and stewed, and a Gypsy band is hired. At the end, the guests pin banknotes onto the bride's dress. At the weddings of Kalderash Rom in America, one guest will collect money for the couple in a long hollowed-out loaf.

Below: This Rom Gypsy bride in France is wearing a European-style wedding-dress, with many silver necklaces and ornaments. She does not look very happy – but then Rom girls are expected to look sad at their wedding because they will have to leave their own family to go and live as the most junior member of their new husband's family.

Below: A table laid for the wedding feast of some Rom Gypsies in California, USA. As well as traditional delicacies they have a European-style three-tiered wedding cake. Several Gypsy groups like to have wedding cakes like these, with many layers, or tiers. Some Irish Travellers now have cakes with up to 20 layers.

The elopement system

In groups like the English Romanichals, where marriage is by elopement, parents make no public plans for their children, even if in private they have their own hopes and ideas. Boys and girls meet each other at the big fairs (see page 26) and when visiting other families. But their parents watch them carefully and make sure a young couple are not left alone together.

When a boy decides to court a girl he passes secret messages to her asking her to run away with him. If she agrees, and they do elope, both sets of parents will try to find them, pretending to be angry even if secretly pleased. Provided, however, that the couple have spent at least one night together away from home, it is generally accepted that they are married. A party is then held to show that everything is forgiven.

Married life in different groups

The time that an English Romanichal couple spend away from their families during their elopement proves that they are grown up and able to live independently. Life is very different for girls from Rom groups. Until they have a baby, or the next son in their husband's family is married, they have to act as a servant to their mother-in-law, and obey her in everything she says.

Nowadays, especially in America and western Europe, girls find it hard to accept this way of life, and many escape back to their own families. Nobody likes divorce, but if it does happen, a *kris* (see page 18) may have to be held to decide whether any or how much of the bride-price should be repaid. But among some Gypsy groups divorce is very rare.

Work

'He knows no bosses, no gaffers. He could make a living out of the dirt of a man's foot. He could make money out of old rope!'
Jimmy Higgins, a Scottish Traveller, 1967

Below: This French Manouche Gypsy is making a basket. Baskets like this, and other items such as chairs, ornaments, and, in the past, carpet-beaters, are sold at local markets, or from door to door.

Notice the caravans behind him. Made to be pulled by horses, they nonetheless have rubber tyres suitable for modern roads, and could easily be converted to be pulled by a motor vehicle.

Almost all Gypsies enjoy being self-employed. They like to be independent in their work, and not have to go to a factory every day, and be ordered about. Their favourite way of working is to offer to do a job for someone, like mending a roof or picking fruit, for example, set a price for the job, do it, and afterwards move on.

Buying and selling

Gypsies' skill at metalwork has made them experts on scrap metal, which they buy from house to house, and sell to scrapyards (some of which are owned by Gypsies). Scrap iron is much cheaper for shipbuilders to use than newly mined iron. Some Gypsies sell items that they have made themselves, such as paper flowers, lace, copper pots, baskets, pegs and charms. Often they also offer to tell their customers' fortunes. Gypsies are also professional musicians or showmen. The circus has many Gypsies like the Italian Sinte family Bouglione. In Latin America, some Rom take film shows to villages without cinemas.

Why the rubbish?

Nowadays the poorest Gypsies are those that still work mainly on farms. Gypsies who live in or near towns can make a good living doing skilled repair work at a cheap price, and also collecting things that house-dwellers no longer want, to recycle them and sell them to someone who can use them. This is often the reason for the piles of what looks like rubbish around Gypsy caravans. In fact it is usually non-Gypsy rubbish which the Gypsies are in the process of clearing up. It can cause problems, however, if the Gypsies are forced to move away before all of the rubbish has been dealt with.

Left: This Rom Gypsy woman is selling flowers at a market in Bucharest, Romania. A large coloured umbrella shades both her and her flowers, which she freshens from time to time with water from the plastic bucket beside her.

Right: These Banjara Gypsies are selling clothes and ornaments at the market in Mapuça in Goa, India. Their colourful skirts and bodices are typical Banjara costume. Notice, too, the heavy jewellery they are wearing.

Below: These Rom in Hungary are working with copper and other metals to make large pots and pans. Note the sizeable tent behind them which they use as a workshed.

One of the Rom Gypsy groups is known as the Kalderash, which is from a Romanian word meaning 'coppersmith'. The Kalderash are probably the most widely spread of all Gypsy groups. Two hundred years ago their ancestors were slave coppersmiths in Romania.

Fairs

'Future partners were found at Appleby Fair or Brough Hill: the news of elopements would usually be soon after . . . When all this was going on, the men would be having their trade.'
Gordon Boswell, an English Romanichal, 1970

Fairs started in the Middle Ages as a chance for people who lived in the country to come to town, usually on some religious festival, to buy and sell horses, cattle, cloth and other goods not normally available. In addition there would often be music, skittles and other amusements. Gypsies found fairs a useful place to do business and to meet one another.

Tourists and horse-trading
Nowadays, with shops everywhere, most people do not need fairs for trading. Some fairs like Cambridge and St Ives have become mere funfairs with roundabouts and swings. Others, like Appleby Fair, have only been kept alive by Gypsies. In 1965 Appleby tried to stop the fair, but Gypsies led by Gordon Boswell resisted and won the right to continue. Horse-trading is still carried on, and tourists flock to see the horses washed in the River Eden. Fairs are, however, chiefly a social gathering, a chance to meet friends and relations not seen for a year. The unmarried can find husbands and wives. Caravans are bought and sold. Thousands of Gypsies treat the fairs as a holiday where for a few days there are as many Gypsies as non-Gypsies in town.

Legends and festivals
In Europe, too, fairs are traditionally linked to religious gatherings. In France, thousands of Calé and other Gypsies go every May to the festival in the Camargue region at Saintes-Maries-de-la-Mer. (There is a legend that the saints' servant, Sara, was a Gypsy.) In the Balkans there are big gatherings on St George's day. Turkish Muslim Rom who join in these festivals call it 'The Day of the Cauldrons'.

Below: Appleby Fair, held every year in the north of England, is a traditional Gypsy fair. Here a Gypsy is showing how fast his horse can pull a small two-wheeled cart. He hopes to sell it to one of the other Gypsies or to the farmers looking on. On the hillside behind there are hundreds of Gypsy caravans, lorries and horse-boxes. This is the romantic face of Gypsy life which tourists come to see.

Food and cleanliness

*'You earn money and say "I'll save this for that and that for this."
We spend a lot of it on food . . . That olla we like to make with its
veal, sausages, cabbage and ground crusts of ham . . .'*
Isabel, a Calo Gitana from Spain, 1970

Below: An Irish Traveller girl washing the family's clothes under very difficult conditions. The Irish Travellers used to be called 'Tinkers' (which means 'tinsmiths') but this has become a word of abuse. Some Gypsies, and some social workers, too, claim that the Irish Travellers are dirty and not 'real' Gypsies. But in fact many of them keep the same kind of cleanliness rules as other Gypsy groups. These rules came originally from the Indian Hindu religion.

When Gypsies are out at work they eat very little. They don't like to go to cafés or restaurants unless they know they are clean. So when they come home, they want a good meal. Whoever has stayed behind feeds each person separately as they come home. Except for big occasions, Gypsy families seldom sit down for a meal together. The children are fed when they are hungry. Usually the mother does the cooking, but if all the women go out, one of the men will have tea ready when they return.

Gypsy cookery

Gypsy cooking varies from country to country. In eastern Europe and Asia lots of hot peppers and spices are used; in western Europe the stews and fries are blander. *Marikli* which are something like Indian chapatis, but with sweet or savoury fillings, are eaten by many Gypsies.

All Gypsies are very particular about their food. Muslim Rom will not eat pork, but love chicken; the Kaale of Finland consider chickens are dirty. Romanichals eat hedgehogs, but other Gypsy groups think that they are unclean.

Hedgehogs

Hedgehogs are caught in the autumn; it is the only time they are fat enough to eat. Dogs are used to sniff them out, and the hedgehogs are then killed with a blow on the nose. Their prickles are singed in the fire and removed with a sharp knife, and then they are cooked in the same way as other small game such as hare or pheasant. Baking a hedgehog rolled in clay is often described as 'Gypsy cooking', but most Gypsies would consider this was dirty. Hedgehog fat is also rubbed on the chest as a cure for colds.

Below: This old photograph shows an English Gypsy family in Kent cooking over a wood fire, *c.* 1945. The cast-iron stewing pot is suspended on a specially made iron bar known as a 'kettle-prop', or *kavvi-saster*.

Bottom of page: This Calé Gitano family are camping on a beach during the great Gypsy gathering at Saintes-Maries-de-la-Mer in France. While the children play in the sand, their parents eat a meal cooked on a modern bottle-gas stove inside their caravan.

Cleanliness and morality

Cleanliness to Gypsies is not just a question of comfort, but of moral standards. These standards are based on the ancient Indian Hindu religion. Different Gypsy groups call filth *marime*, *mochadi* or *melalo*, and some are stricter about it than others, but all think that a dirty person not only endangers everyone's health, but also the dignity of Gypsies. A Gypsy believed to be unclean will be avoided like someone guilty of a crime.

Washing

Above all, Gypsies pay particular attention to hygiene when handling food. They insist that cups, plates and teatowels are washed in a separate bowl from clothes, and that a third bowl is kept for washing themselves. Separate bowls are used for washing the floor or feeding animals. All animals have to live outside. A cup that falls on the ground or is licked by an animal will immediately be smashed and thrown away. Some Rom even use different bowls for washing men's and women's clothes. Non-Gypsies often think that Gypsies are dirty – when they see children playing with scrap metal, for example. But most Gypsies consider non-Gypsies dirty when they let dogs run about the house, and wash teatowels in the same machine as their clothes!

The Khereskero

Whatever mess there may be outside, keeping the home clean and tidy is important. The Arliski Rom of Yugoslavia say that a spirit called the *Khereskero* lives behind the door of the house and checks that everything is kept clean. If it is not, or if he hears idle chatter about him, he will punish the family with bad luck.

Religion

'I come from a large family, of honourable life and manners. My strict upbringing gave me an intense desire to see the Romani people live a morally clean life.'
Stevo Demeter, Kalderash Rom preacher, Paris

Right: At the Catholic festival at Saintes-Maries-de-la-Mer in France, held every May, statues of saints are taken in procession from the church to the sea. Thousands of Gypsies and tourists watch the procession.

Bottom of page: Catholic Gypsies light candles in the church at Saintes-Maries.

Below: Three Gypsy pastors from the Gypsy Evangelical Church are about to baptise a Sinte Gypsy girl in a lake at Mannheim in Germany, as a sign of her new Christian life.

Gypsies have no one religion. Their travels have probably left them freer to think for themselves than people who stay in one place. Some are superstitious, some are not. Gypsies brought from India not so much a set of beliefs about God and the afterlife, as a way of living. Their attitude towards cleanliness (see page 29) is an example of this.

Islam and Christianity

Gypsies came into contact with Islam in Turkey and with Christianity in Europe. Some became sincere believers and even clergymen. Many Muslim Gypsies keep the Ramadan fast, eating only at night for a month each year. Many Catholic and Orthodox Gypsies go regularly to mass; in Rome the Pope has received Gypsies. In England Gypsy Rodney Smith (1860–1947) became a famous preacher. It was difficult, however, for Gypsies to join churches which opposed their nomadic and self-employed way of life.

A Gypsy Church

In the 1950s, a new Christian group started in France, called the Gypsy Evangelical Church. It said that Gypsies could be better Gypsies if they were also sincere Christians. The Church organizes enthusiastic services. They use Gypsy music and the Romanes language in their hymns and prayers. They are led by Gypsy pastors, who have learnt to read and spent a few months in Bible college, but still have to make their own living by trading; they are not paid for preaching. The movement has spread like wildfire in some countries. Many Gypsy pastors also work to get better legal and educational rights for their people.

Language, story and song

'It is true, as the Lovara Rom say, "Amari shib si amari zor" – "Our language is our strength".'
Dr Ian Hancock, a Gypsy and Professor at the University of Texas (Austin), 1975

Gypsies love to sit in the open air around a wood fire. Often their talk will turn to old stories and legends. As well as their own songs and stories, Gypsies have preserved much otherwise forgotten non-Gypsy folklore. Here is a story told by some Kalderash Rom:

The goatskin tea-bottle
Once upon a time a baby boy was born to a Gypsy family. He was rather sickly, and his parents were afraid that he might die. An old lady came to the family's caravan to look at him and see what his chances were. Afterwards she shook her head grimly, saying to the parents: 'Your son is going to die.' The father was desperate.

'What can I do to stop him dying?' he asked.

'There is only one thing you can do,' said the old lady. 'Take a goatskin bottle, and fill it with tea. Then take one of the tins in which you make clay bricks, and put the goatskin bottle inside. Pack clay all round the bottle. Leave it to dry in the sun, and when the brick has been baked, keep it underneath the young boy's bed.'

The boy grew up into a healthy young man. The family travelled far and wide. One day they came to a dry and windswept desert. The young man fell dangerously ill and began calling out for water, saying that he was dying of thirst. The family had no water, but the father suddenly remembered the goatskin bottle of tea hidden in the brick which he had stored beneath his son's bed.

He took out the brick and cracked it open. Then he tried to open the goatskin bottle, but it was so old and brittle that it broke in his hands and the tea flowed from it into the dust beneath his feet.

The young man died, and his family wept for him. But the patch of earth where the tea had fallen stayed damp. When the Gypsies dug the soil on the wet patch, they found a spring from which they were able to make a well.

Afterwards, passing travellers told the story, saying: 'A Gypsy died here, but where he died there is now a well from which anyone who comes by may drink.'

The Gypsy language
Originally this story was told in the Gypsies' own language, Romanes. Gypsies brought this language from India. People who know Indian languages such as Hindi or Gujerati can often recognize Romani words like *pani* (water), *kalo* (black), and the numbers *yek*, *dui*, *trin*, *star*, *panch* (1,2,3,4,5). While travelling from India, the Gypsies added to their vocabulary words from the languages of the countries through which they passed, especially Persian, Greek and Romanian. The history of their travels can be traced by studying Romanes.

Between 2 and 5 million Gypsies speak dialects of Romanes, complete with their own grammar. The poem on the right is by a modern Czechoslovak poet, a Rom called Frantishek Demeter. It was written specially for children, and published in a collection of Gypsy poems.

Gitara
*Chin cha mange gitarica
miri dayori lachori,
mai dikhesa sa bashava
gilavava gilori . . .*

*Shukares me bashavava
o hangi sa chivkerava
sar o Roma shunena
savore yon khelena.*

The guitar
O please just buy me a guitar
dear little mother of mine,
then you will see how I will play
and sing my songs sublime . . .

I will play so beautifully
from chord to chord entranced,
the whole Romani people will hear
and everyone will dance.

Right: The famous guitarist Manitas de Plata is a Calo Gypsy from the south of France. His name means 'Little hands of silver'. He has adopted traditional Flamenco music to create a popular and successful style. The caravan on which he is sitting is not actually being lived in by Gypsies, but it makes a romantic backdrop for the picture.

Pogadi jib

There are many different dialects and varieties of Romanes. About one million Gypsies, including the English Romanichals, the Hungarian Romungri and many French Manouche mix Romani words with the language of the country in which they live. The English Gypsies call this kind of dialect *pogadi jib* which means 'broken tongue'. Even though 'English Romany' is mostly English, for example, non-Gypsies cannot understand it.

The song on the right, 'The Gypsy Gentleman', is in *pogadi jib*. You can see there a few Romani words among the English. Almost all English Gypsy children know this song. The chorus suddenly breaks into fast Romanes – just like a Gypsy horse-dealer at the market might do when he doesn't want any non-Gypsies there to *in what he's pukkering* (know what he's saying).

Romani writing

Today there are not only traditional songs and stories in Romanes. Gypsies have begun to use their language to write books, magazines and newspapers. Until this century almost no Romanes was written down, and very few Gypsies could read or write it. Now a Yugoslav Rom, Jusuf Shaip, has even published a Romani grammar.

Some Romani writers have called for all the dialects to be reunited, but this is difficult. Every group of Gypsies, large or small, tends to think its own dialect is best. But as more is written in Romanes, and more Gypsies from different countries meet, they are realizing the value that every dialect holds for the people who live, work, sing and tell stories in it.

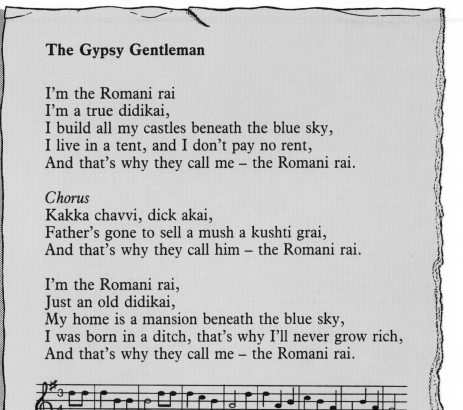

The Gypsy Gentleman

I'm the Romani rai
I'm a true didikai,
I build all my castles beneath the blue sky,
I live in a tent, and I don't pay no rent,
And that's why they call me – the Romani rai.

Chorus
Kakka chavvi, dick akai,
Father's gone to sell a mush a kushti grai,
And that's why they call him – the Romani rai.

I'm the Romani rai,
Just an old didikai,
My home is a mansion beneath the blue sky,
I was born in a ditch, that's why I'll never grow rich,
And that's why they call me – the Romani rai.

fast   slow

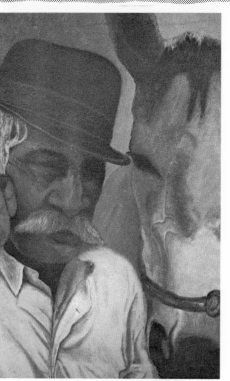

Above: This song is sung by nearly all English Gypsy children. It shows the way the 'English Romany' *pogadi jib* works. There are only a few words of Romanes – but you cannot get the full flavour of the song without knowing them. *Rai* means 'lord'; *didakai* literally means a 'look-'ere fellow', a rough ignorant person. (It does *not*, as some non-Gypsy books claim, mean 'half-breed'.) *Kakka chavvi*, *dick akai*, means 'Quiet boy, look here'; *mush* means 'man'; *kushti grai* means 'good horse'.

The song is full of irony: it shows how sometimes it's romantic to be a Gypsy; and how at other times, for some Gypsies, it's pretty tough not to have a permanent home or much money.

Left: This painting of an old man with a horse is by the Hungarian Rom painter Jozsef Kiss, who was born in 1921. The painting was exhibited along with many others by self-taught Romani artists in June 1979, at an exhibition in Budapest organized by Gypsies. The painting uses deep browns and oranges to show the warm friendship between the '*Romani Rai*' and his '*kushti grai*'.

Music

'Gypsies express in their music their grief and their joy . . . Music accompanies their life from earliest childhood until death itself.'
Dr Jan Cibula, president, 1978 World Romani Congress

Below: This medal was struck in memory of Django Reinhardt. He was given a guitar when he was nine, and as well as traditional music began to play American-style jazz. When he was 18 his caravan caught fire and he was in hospital for 18 months. He lost two fingers from his left hand and had to work out new ways of playing. He composed jazz pieces based on Gypsy songs, and became famous all over the world.

Bottom of page: Gypsy Flamenco for tourists in a cave near Granada.

Dr Cibula, a Lovari Rom, is a remarkable violinist as well as being a doctor. He explained: 'Often it's only among ourselves, at family gatherings, that Gypsies play their own true music – the old Gypsy songs, heard again and again as we travelled, helping us to put up with our troubles, to tell out our hopes and emotions, to complain of the lack of understanding by the Gaje (non-Gypsies).'

At feasts and gatherings someone will start singing, sometimes an old song in Romanes, sometimes a modern 'pop' song. Gypsies who cannot read have very good memories and can often remember all of a new song after hearing it just once – on the radio, for example. Each Gypsy group has its own musical style, mixing elements brought from India with local music to create something new.

Folk music and professional music

Gypsies make many kinds of 'folk' music for their own amusement. But if they want to earn money, Gypsy musicians have to become professional, and play the sort of music customers want. The three most famous styles of professional Gypsy music are those of the Hungarian Romungri bands, the Flamenco of Spain, and most recently the Gypsy jazz of French and German Sinte and Manouche.

Gypsy jazz

The founder of Gypsy jazz was a Manouche, Django Reinhardt (1910–53), one of the greatest of jazz musicians. Today many bands record his style of music and every Manouche boy with a guitar tries to imitate it. So Django Reinhardt was not just a great professional musician; he also gave his people a new style of folk music.

Below: This Hungarian Gypsy band is playing in a famous restaurant in Budapest. As well as a violinist (not in the picture) who leads the band, there is a guitar, a double bass and a 'cymbalon', a stringed instrument hit with hammers by the player who sits behind it. Over 300 years ago in Hungary, Gypsy violinists were employed to play at the court of princes, and in army regiments. Today they have their own trade union recognized by the government. Their music is very different from Flamenco which originated in Spanish Calo folk-dances.

Sickness and death

'When there is a death or an illness, all Gypsies get together, whether they have to walk, sell everything, no matter what. It's a sign of respect.'
American Rom, early 1970s

Below: A table laid out for a *pomana* or funeral feast for a dead Rom Gypsy in California, USA. A large photograph of the dead woman has been placed at one end of the table, surrounded by flowers, with a candle and food set out before it. At least three and perhaps even more such feasts will be held, so that the Rom can show their proper respect to the dead person. Relatives will come from a great distance, even from other countries, to be present, so a *pomana* is also an important family reunion.

When they are sick Gypsies often prefer to rely on their own knowledge, and to cure themselves. Some doctors refuse to treat them out of prejudice, and anyway Gypsies are not always certain that doctors are clean. In fact, until standards of hygiene improved in the nineteenth century, hospitals were dirty, and Gypsy health standards often higher. Gypsies used to make medicines from herbs, as did many country people. Nettle tea was a tonic. Broom-leaf tea or dandelion salad were used for kidney complaints. Nowadays, however, many Gypsies buy their medicines from chemists and have a greater trust in doctors.

Funerals

To relatives and friends, death brings great grief. The body itself is usually given a religious burial, but a dead Gypsy's possessions are smashed, and his clothes burnt.

Gypsies do not like to inherit from the dead. They give away most of their money before they die, and the rest is buried with them. Among nomadic groups even the caravan or tent of the dead person is burnt; not to do so is a sign of poverty.

The pomana

American Kalderash and Machvaya Rom do not burn their houses, but like Rom groups in Europe they have a special triple feast, the *pomana*, which is held three days, nine days and six weeks after someone's death. A Rom from a different group who did not know the dead person is given new clothes similar to those the dead person used to wear. He is addressed by the dead person's name, and acts out his part at the feast. This enables the ghost to enjoy the food and the respect of his family.

Burning caravans

Recently an English Gypsy of about 40 was killed in a road accident. His widow and three children were cared for by relatives while his new caravan and two lorries worth £15,000 were burnt. 'Suppose we sold his lorry,' his brother said, 'and then one day we saw it driven up the road; how would we feel?' Before the burning there was a big church funeral.

Joy and sadness

The poem below, by the Yugoslav Rom poet, Rajko Durich, sums up the attitudes of Gypsies to life and death. It is quite a difficult poem to understand; a lot of meaning is packed into just a few words. The poet says that both life and death are a mixture of sadness and joy:

Moonlight

O chonut asal amen . . .
. . . Te o chonut korhavola
te amen dikhasa
kon vakarela

Kaj e phak e rovimase
thaj e asamase
ka arakhadon

The moon smiles
down on us
around the fire
we weep

Our crying flies up
among the moonbeams floating down
heaven smells our tears
we sense the beams
If the moon is blinded
we can see
who is speaking . . .
With one wing of tears
and one of laughter
we take off to meet him

Asia

Gypsies are not the only nomads in Asia. There are also 'pastoral' nomads who make their living herding cattle. Sometimes the two groups travel together. In Iran, the Ghorbati Gypsies are protected by pastoral nomads, and do metalwork both for them and for the townspeople.

Different countries, different names
Gypsies who stayed in the Middle East called themselves Jats or Zotts. The Arabs called them Nawar. In some countries Gypsies' names reflect their previous travels. In Egypt they are called 'Halebi' (people from Aleppo). There is also a small Rom group of singers and dancers, the Ghagar, who were forced into Egypt by the Turks who then ruled the area.

India, the mother country
In 1966 Pandit Nehru's daughter, Mrs Indira Gandhi, Prime Minister of India, told an Indian Gypsy group, the Banjara Seva Sangh: 'My father once said that if he were given a choice, he would like to choose for himself the nomadic life of the Banjaras and roam about like a free soul . . . We would not want you to lose your separate identity and characteristic way of life; these lend colour to the national life.' As their mother country India now supports Gypsies all over the world in their fight for a better life.

Right: This vivacious dance is being performed by Indian Hampi nomads. Note that like the Banjara and other Indian Gypsy groups they have their own style of dress, quite different from the sari Indian women normally wear. Educated members of these nomadic groups used to abandon their native dress; but in the past twenty years there has been a movement among them to secure a better life without losing their identity.

Gypsies in America

'The greatest strength of the Gypsies is their invisibility . . . the merge into the mass of strangers on the street.'
Ronald Lee, Canadian Romanichal Gypsy novelist, 1971

Below: This Rom Gypsy is standing in front of her fortune-telling parlour, or *ofisa* as it is called in Romanes. To attract non-Gypsy customers it advertises 'Astrology' in the window, and displays religious statuettes. But, whatever the props used, whether crystal balls, palmistry or tarot cards, Gypsy fortune-telling remains firmly based in commonsense, psychology and guesswork. If a customer comes in dressed in a good suit, it is usually safe to tell him he'll soon be going on a business trip, or meeting a new friend.

Europeans first settled in America in the sixteenth century, at the same time as the great persecution of Gypsies in Europe. The rich among the colonists could invest their new wealth in trade; the poor could escape there to find a living and new land.

America was also a place to send convicted criminals: they were made to work for the free colonists. Among these convicts Calo Gypsies were taken by the Spaniards to central and south America, while the British took Romanichals to New England and the West Indies.

Gypsy refugees

In the eighteenth century some Gypsy refugees escaping from Holland chartered their own boats. One boat sank, but the others reached the hills of Pennsylvania to live among the Dutch-speaking people there.

Irish Travellers went to the southern United States at the beginning of the nineteenth century to escape the great famine in Ireland. They traded mules to both sides in the American civil war. Today they still speak the same Irish Traveller language (the *Gammon*) as Irish Travellers in Ireland, England and Australia.

Land of the free

The biggest wave of immigrants to America came at the end of the nineteenth century (see map page 16). Transport across the Atlantic became cheaper, and stories of a free open country, where everyone had an equal chance to get rich, spread through Europe. Gypsies from western Europe left the depressed countryside in hundreds; East European Gypsies, just a generation away from slavery, poured across to the New World in their thousands.

Below: In February 1970 a special school was started in Richmond, California, for the Kalderash, Kuneshti and Machvaya Rom living there. It was run on a voluntary basis, with some help from social workers. Work was based on Gypsies' own stories and songs.

Bottom of page: A group of well-to-do Gypsies. For them America has been a land of opportunity. Most non-Gypsies, unless told, would not realize that these men are Gypsies.

The hidden Americans

Today in North America there are immigrants from almost every European Gypsy group. But apart from Rom fortune-tellers and a few Hungarian Romungri musicians, they do not advertise themselves as Gypsies, for fear of prejudice. In 1969 one local politician said that he could not help the migrant (nomadic) farmworkers to whom farmers were paying low wages because: 'They are Gypsies, they don't like to work.' So Gypsies doing farmwork pretend to be French-Canadians, or Mexicans, anything to avoid prejudice. America has so many immigrants that Gypsies do not stand out. Travelling is also easier than in Europe. Besides Gypsies, over 250,000 North Americans and their families travel from farm to farm looking for work. There are many cheap caravan sites and motels, and cheap houses to rent in the slums.

Problems

Some of the poorer and more recent Rom immigrants have encountered problems. Their old metalwork trades are not in demand, and if they cannot read and write it is hard for them to find work. Some do not like to send their children to non-Gypsy schools. They rely more and more for a living on fortune-telling, welfare payments, and sometimes crime. This brings them into contact with social workers and the police. They are written about in newspapers and books, which often present a few poor or criminal Rom as if typical of all Gypsies. This is very worrying to the Rom community, and to compensate they hold the *kris* (see page 16) more frequently than the European Rom, and insist very strictly on the cleanliness rules.

The way ahead

'Opre Roma! Rise up, Romanies!... Crouching in wet tents and crowded shanties from Stockholm to Barcelona, half a million have-nots have nothing to lose. For some 4 million Rom in south-east Europe... the prize is dignity.'
Grattan Puxon, World Romani Congress, 1971

Below: A peaceful but illegal encampment of Gypsies in France. The notice says: 'It is illegal for nomads or caravanners to stop here.' By the 1960s in western Europe there were very few places left where Gypsies could camp legally.

Bottom of page: An eviction of Gypsies near Birmingham in England, in 1973. 'Private detectives' were hired to tow the caravans away. Dozens of police came to protect these 'private detectives'. The operation cost thousands of pounds.

The first stirrings of modern Gypsy organization in eastern Europe after the 1917 Russian Revolution were largely killed off by Hitler and Stalin. During the Second World War, however, in Bulgaria, Yugoslavia and other countries, Gypsies fought as guerillas. They joined up with Communist groups to throw out the old rulers who supported Hitler. After 1945 Communist governments provided housing and education, but there was often still local prejudice.

The World Romani Congress
During the 1960s the International Romani Committee in Paris (see page 18) encouraged Gypsies to fight for education, and for sites to park their caravans. In 1971, at Easter, Gypsy organizations from East and West European countries came together at a boarding school near London to hold the first World Romani Congress. Never had Gypsies from such different backgrounds all been together. Educated Rom, lawyers and doctors from Czechoslovakia and Yugoslavia ate in the school diningroom with English Gypsy scrap-metal dealers and Romani preachers from France and Finland. They demanded recognition of their identity and language, and compensation for Gypsies murdered during the war.

The United Nations
After the first World Romani Congress, India began to support the Gypsy cause at the United Nations. In 1978 a much bigger second World Romani Congress was held in Geneva. There were delegates from 26 countries in America, Europe and Asia. In 1979 the United Nations recognized the Romani Union, set up by Congress leaders.

Below: A crying Gypsy boy tries in vain to stop a 'private detective' who came to evict him from his caravan home, Birmingham, 1973. Among those who resisted this eviction was Grattan Puxon, now Joint Secretary of the World Romani Congress.

Bottom of page: A session of the 1978 World Romani Congress in Geneva. The six delegates at the front table on the left are English Gypsies. The banner at the back says *Sa Roma Prala* – 'All Gypsies are brothers'. Television cameras record the occasion.

Political problems

The World Romani Congress has sometimes been criticised, especially by social workers who feel that Gypsies should not keep themselves separate, but should be absorbed into the rest of the population. People say that the Congress delegates are too well-educated to know what all the uneducated Gypsies really want, and that the leaders waste too much time quarrelling among themselves. Some say that they are trying too hard to protect Gypsies from change; others that they are forcing too much change too quickly. But these criticisms are not really valid. Educated Gypsies feel they must work for their own people. And if something is important, it is worth arguing about. Arguments between leaders do not mean that they are not sincere.

A test of freedom

Gypsies are not like other groups of people who have a land to call their own. Gypsies always have to live in the world of non-Gypsies. Some are rich, some are poor. Sometimes they disguise themselves from non-Gypsies so that no-one but themselves knows who they are, and even their children may forget their Gypsy ancestry. Sometimes they try flamboyantly to live up to the public image of Gypsies. If people say they want 'real' Gypsy music, the Gypsies give them the popular idea of it. Either way, Gypsy culture is continually being changed. This does not mean that the Gypsies are any less independent or attached to their own family life. They will continue to show the world the possibility of not being tied down by one job, one boss, or one place. Their freedom is a measure of the freedom of us all.

Things to do

Bender tents

Bender tents, used by Gypsies for hundreds of years, are still home for some today. Smaller ones are also used as dog kennels. To make one you will need: eight fresh-cut sticks of wood; one double length stick of wood; some old sacks, tarpaulins or blankets; string; some large safety pins; and about eight heavy stones.

1. Choose somewhere where you can push the sticks into the ground in the pattern shown above.

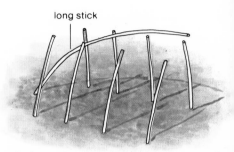

long stick

2. Insert the sticks securely in the ground, with pairs facing each other and the long one at the end.

Paper flowers

Many Gypsies make paper flowers to sell. There are many different types. Some are very complicated and require great skill. But you can easily make a paper flower by following the instructions on the right. You will need: a few pieces of crepe paper; some cotton thread; and a small stick (possibly a green wire pipe-cleaner).

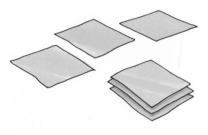

1. Cut the crepe tissue paper into squares and then place them one on top of another in a pile.

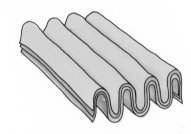

2. Keeping the squares together, fold them into a concertina shape, as shown, in small, even folds.

Marikli

This type of Gypsy bread is like the Indian *chapati*. Poorer Gypsies cook it as shown here; others roll it around a savoury filling such as spinach, or a sweet filling like jam. The necessary ingredients are: 8 oz (300 gm) wholewheat flour; 1 teaspoon salt; 5 fluid oz (0.14 litres) warm water; some olive or sunflower oil; a little butter.

1. Sift the flour and salt into a bowl. Make a well in the centre, add the water and mix thoroughly.

2. Turn out the dough onto a lightly floured surface and knead it until it feels rubbery. Leave it to stand for a few minutes.

A model Gypsy caravan

On page 12, there is a picture of a bow-top caravan. With the following materials you could make a simplified model of one. You will need: some thin cardboard for the sides and base; some thicker cardboard for the wheels; two thin sticks, such as cocktail sticks; glue (and/or sticky tape); a felt tip pen; assorted oil paints in different colours.

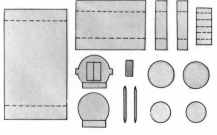

1. From the thin cardboard make one rectangle, two folds, and three strips. Cut out four wheels from the thicker cardboard.

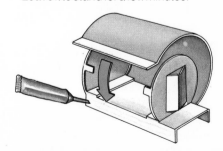

2. Fold the roof over the base and glue the two together. Also attach the sides to it with glue.

3. Bend the four pairs over and tie them together with string. Attach the long one through the knots.

4. Place the cover on top of the bent sticks, pinning it together all the way round with the safety pins.

5. Weigh down the ends of the cover with stones. If it rains put more material over the entrance.

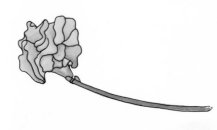

3. Bend the concertina in the middle into a V-shape, and tie a piece of cotton tightly round the bottom.

4. Loosen the folds of paper, tearing some a little at the top, so that the result looks like a flower.

5. Tie the end of the cotton onto a stick. (To make your flower last longer, dip it in melted candle wax coloured with red ink.)

3. Divide the dough into eight and sprinkle with sunflower or olive oil. Then, on a lightly floured surface, roll out thinly.

4. Cook, one at a time, in a lightly oiled frying pan. After a few minutes the surface will bubble.

5. Turn over and cook for another minute until a light golden colour. Serve warm (adding some butter if you prefer).

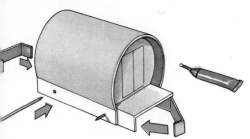

3. Glue on the bottom flaps and make holes through them for the wheel axles. Make a hole for the chimney.

4. Draw spokes on the wheels and attach them. Concertina the cardboard strip to make the steps, and insert the chimney.

5. Decorate your caravan with the paints, trying to follow the style of the one on page 12 as much as you can.

Reference

The Romani language

The word *Romani* itself is an adjective, the feminine form of *Romano* which means 'Gypsy'. One speaks of the 'Romani language' because *jib* ('language' in Romanes) is a feminine noun. *Romani* should not be used as a noun or an adverb. The adverb is *Romanes* ('in Gypsy fashion') which is also sometimes used as a noun. Thus it is correct to say 'I speak the Romani language' or 'I speak Romanes', but *not*, strictly, 'I speak Romani' (although, in fact, some English Gypsies do say this).

Romani verbs are conjugated; the present tense of *dikhava* (I see) goes as follows:

Me dikhav(a)	I see
Tu dikhes(a)	You see
Ov dikhel(a)	He sees
Ame dikhas(a)	We see
Tume dikhen(a)	You see
On dikhen(a)	They see

In the English Romani (or 'Romany') *pogadi jib* this is changed to I dick, you dick, he dicks, we dick, you dick, they dick.

Glossary

A. ROMANI WORDS

Arliski. A Muslim Balkan Rom group.
Banjara. An Indian Gypsy group.
Boyash. Name given to Romanian-speaking Gypsies by Rom groups.
Gajo, plural **Gajé.** Non-Gypsy.
Gaujo, plural **Gaujos.** Non-Gypsy in the English Romani dialect.
Ghagar. An Egyptian Gypsy group.
Kalderash. A Rom group (from the Romanian word for 'coppersmith').
Kalo, Kaalo, Calo plural **Kalé, Calé.** Black; also used by some Gypsies to mean 'Gypsy'.
Khereskero. Household spirit.
Kris. Rom tribunal or court.
Lovari. A Rom group.
Manouche, Manush. A man; name used by a French Gypsy group.

Marime, Melalo, Mochadi. Filthy.
Mush. Man (English Romani dialect).
Naik. A Banjara headman.
Pani. Water.
Pogadi jib. Broken tongue (used to describe Romani dialects mixed with other languages).
Pomana. Rom funeral feast.
Rom. Man, husband; also used by some East European groups to mean 'Gypsy'.
Romanichal. A Gypsy man (West European dialects only).
Shib, Jib. Tongue, language.
Sinte. A Gypsy group in Germany and Italy and elsewhere.
Zott. The Gypsies of the Middle East.

B. NON-GYPSY WORDS

Bride-price. Money paid by the groom's father to the bride's father at a wedding.
Caste. Division in the Indian class system (see page 4).
Elopement. When two people run away to get married.
Gitano, feminine **Gitana.** Gypsy (in Spanish).
Gypsy. Word used in English to refer to the Romani, Zott, Banjara and other semi-nomadic peoples of Indian origin.
Halebi. Egyptian word for Gypsies (literally, people from Aleppo).
Kowli. Middle Eastern word for Gypsies.
Nawar. Arabic word for the Zott Gypsies.
Nazi. Abbreviation for the National Socialist party which ruled Germany between 1933 and 1945. They wanted to exterminate Gypsies and Jews.
Nomad. Person who regularly moves his home to make his living in different places.
Pastor. Leader or clergyman of an evangelical church.
Ramadan. Month during which devout Muslims do not eat during the day. Many Gypsies in south-east Europe and the Middle East keep this fast.
Tinker, Tinkler. Irish and Scottish word used to refer to Gypsies or 'Travellers' (literally, tinsmith). It has now become a term of abuse and is no longer much used.

Estimates of Gypsy Population

Eastern Europe

Yugoslavia	750,000–1,000,000
Romania	500,000–700,000
Hungary	350,000–600,000
USSR	200,000–500,000
Bulgaria	400,000–500,000
Czechoslovakia	300,000–400,000
Poland	60,000–70,000
Albania	60,000–70,000
East Germany	20,000–50,000

Total: Between 2½ and 4 million.

Western Europe

Spain	500,000–700,000
France	100,000–230,000
Italy	60,000–100,000
Portugal	30,000–90,000
West Germany	50,000–80,000
Britain	80,000–110,000
Greece	50,000–90,000
Netherlands	40,000–50,000
Belgium	10,000–16,000
Ireland	12,000–25,000
Switzerland	12,000–25,000
Austria	5,000–11,000
Sweden	5,000–10,000
Finland	6,000–8,000
Norway	4,000–5,000
Denmark	2,000–4,000

Total: Between 1 and 1½ million.

Other countries

Turkey	100,000–500,000
Egypt	100,000–200,000
Middle East	1–2 million
North America	1–1½ million
South America	½–1 million
Pakistan	1–2 million
India	10–20 million
Others	under ½ million

The above figures include both settled and nomadic Gypsies. So, depending on how you define Gypsy, the world Gypsy population is between 17 and 33 million. Of these around ½ million European and 2–3 million non-European Gypsies are nomadic. There are around 4–5 million Rom, and perhaps a million each in the groups referred to in this book as Romanichals and Calé. Nobody really knows how many Asian Gypsies there are.

Important dates

Before **AD 400.** Some Indians become nomadic craftsmen and entertainers.

430-443. 10,000 nomadic Indian musicians taken to Persia.

820-834. Zott state established on the banks of the River Tigris.

c.1000. Gypsies reach the Byzantine Empire (modern Greece and Turkey).

c.1300. Gypsy groups begin to be enslaved in south-east Europe.

1383. Gypsies recorded in Hungary.

1407. Gypsies recorded in Germany.

1419. Gypsies recorded in France.

1447. Gypsies recorded in Spain.

1501. Gypsies recorded in Russia.

1505. Gypsies recorded in Scotland.

1530. First English law expelling Gypsies.

1554. First English law making it a capital offence to be a Gypsy; similar laws also passed in other countries.

1761. Maria Theresa, Empress of Austria, passes first laws in Europe trying to settle and reform Gypsies.

1856. Final abolition of Gypsy slavery in Romania; large-scale emigrations to western Europe and America.

1925-9. Soviet Romani Writers' Association founded, then suppressed; Moscow Gypsy Theatre started. (It is still going.)

1930. Michael Kwiek recognized as King of the Gypsies by Polish government.

1933. Gypsy Congress at Bucharest. Nazis come to power in Germany.

1939-45. Second World War; Nazi genocide of Gypsies and Jews.

1959. World Gypsy Community founded in Paris; changes name to International Romani Committee after ban by French government, 1965.

1966. British Gypsy Council founded.

1968. Caravan Sites Act passed in England.

1971. First World Romani Congress.

1976. Romani Festival held at Chandigarh, India; Mrs Indira Gandhi pledges support.

1978. Second World Romani Congress; the Romani Union founded.

1979. Romani Union given consultative status by the United Nations.

How to find out more

Gypsies, Their Life and Their Customs by Martin Block (AMS Pr., 1977). Translated by B. Kuczynski and D. Taylor. Illustrated.

Nights and Days on the Gypsy Trail: Through Andalusia and Other Mediterranean Shores by Irving H. Brown (AMS Pr., 1977). Illustrated.

Gypsy Idyll: A Personal Experience Among the Romanies by Rowena Farre (Vanguard, no date). Illustrated.

Gypsies by Howard Greenfield (Crown, 1977). Illustrated, good for older children.

Gypsies by John W. Hornby (Walck, 1967). From the Byways Library series. Illustrated; good for children in grades 4 to 7.

The Destiny of Europe's Gypsies by D. Kendrick and G. Puxton (Basic, 1972). The full story of Gypsies' suffering under the Nazis.

Tales of the Real Gypsy by Paul Kester (Gale, 1971). Reprinting of the 1897 edition.

Gypsies by Bart McDowell and the National Geographic Society (Special Publications Series, 1970). Available only from National Geographic.

Gypsies: The Hidden Americans by Anne Sutherland (Free Press, 1975)

Sources of Information

World Romani Congress Secretariat, odos Dimokritou 19, Akropoli, Salonika, Greece.

Books and literature can be obtained from *Romanestan Publications,* 82 Eversham Road, London, England EL54AJ.

Periodicals

Traveller Education, published by the National Gypsy Education Council, from Romanestan Publications (see above).

Libraries

Trinity College Library, 300 Summit St., Hartford, Conn.

Newberry Library, 60 W. Walton St., Chicago, Ill.

New York Public Library, Research Library, General Research and Humanities Division, Fifth Ave. and 42 St., New York, N.Y.

Acknowledgments

Dr. D.S. Kenrick advised on the text. B. Hurley arranged the music on page 33. The Smith family taught the author to make a bender tent, and the Doran family to make paper flowers (page 44). The recipe for *marikli* was given by Sanije Ibrahim Puxon (page 44). The poem on page 32 comes from *Romske Pisne,* ed. M. Hubschmannova and V. Sloup (Kulturni Dum, Prague, 1979). The poem on page 37 comes from *Bi Kheresko Bi Limoresko* by Rajko Durich (Nolit, Belgrade, 1979). Quotations not acknowledged in the text were taken from *Gypsy Politics and Social Change* by T. A. Acton (Routledge, 1974), *Qué Gitano* by B. B. Qintana and L. G. Floyd (Holt Rinehart, 1972) and *Gypsies, The Hidden Americans* by A. Sutherland (Tavistock, 1975).

Photographs

Key: T (top); B (bottom); L (left); R (right); C (centre)

Alan Hutchinson: cover, 4(B), 21(T)
Robert Harding/Trevor Wood: 2–3
Photographie Giraudon: 8(B)
Denis Harvey: 12(T), 13
Ghetto Fighters House, Israel: 14
Popperfoto: 15 (T and B)
Alain Dagbert/Viva: 18
Janine Wiedel: 19(T)
Dick Scott-Stewart: 19(B)
Photo Desjeux: 20, 30(B), 31
Rex Features: 21(B)
Mateo Maximoff: 22, 30(T), 42(T)
Lyn Smith: 23, 36, 40, 41(T and B)
Explorer/R. Claquin: 24(T), 29(T)
Chris Niedenthal: 24(B)
Rex Features/Kallen Fury: 25(T)
Robert Harding: 25(B), 38–39
Homer Sykes: 26–27
Ruan O'Lochlain/Aspect: 28
John Topham: 29(B), 35
Lucien Clergue: 32
John Topham/Fotogram: 34
Marion Schweitzer/Rex: 37
Dick Worrall: 42(B), 43(T)
Thomas Acton: 43(B)
Macdonald Educational files: 8(T) 33(B)

Artists

B. L. Kearley/Donald Harley: 5, 6-7, 9, 10–11
B. L. Kearley/Jeremy Gower: 4(T), 16–17
Tony Payne: 8(T), 34(T)
Hayward Art Group: 12(B), 33(T), 44–5

Index